TO:

FROM:

for you...

Made in the USA
Columbia, SC
15 March 2024

33106573R00068